MW01155345

wild canines

DINGOES

Elaine McKinnon

PowerKiDS press™

New York

Published in 2017 by The Rosen Publishing Group, Inc.
29 East 21st Street, New York, NY 10010

Copyright © 2017 by The Rosen Publishing Group, Inc.

All rights reserved. No part of this book may be reproduced in any form without permission in writing from the publisher, except by a reviewer.

First Edition

Editor: Caitie McAneney
Book Design: Tanya Dellaccio

Photo Credits: Cover (dingo), p. 12 FiledIMAGE/Shutterstock.com; cover (landscape background) Jeffrey M. Frank/Shutterstock.com; cover, pp. 3, 4, 6–8, 10,12, 14–16, 18, 20, 22–24 (background) Iliveinoctober/Shutterstock.com; pp. 4, 13, 17 Auscape/UIG/Getty Images; pp. 5, 11 Nicholas Toh/Shutterstock.com; p. 6 Susan Schmitz/Shutterstock.com; pp. 7 (top), 19 John Carnemolla/Shutterstock.com; pp. 7 (bottom), 15 (top) Susan Flashman/Shutterstock.com; p. 9 Julie Fletcher/Getty Images; p. 15 (bottom) Christian Musat/Shutterstock.com; p. 21 Tiberius Dinu/Shutterstock.com; p. 22 SF photo/Shutterstock.com.

Cataloging-in-Publication Data

Title: Dingoes / Elaine McKinnon.
Description: New York : PowerKids Press, 2017. | Series: Wild canines | Includes index.
Identifiers: ISBN 9781499420197 (pbk.) | ISBN 9781499420210 (library bound) | ISBN 9781499420203 (6 pack)
Subjects: LCSH: Dingo–Juvenile literature.
Classification: LCC QL737.C22 M35 2017 | DDC 599.77′2–d23

Manufactured in the United States of America

CPSIA Compliance Information: Batch #BS16PK: For Further Information contact Rosen Publishing, New York, New York at 1-800-237-9932

CONTENTS

Australia's Wild Dog

Australia is home to an amazing canine called the dingo. Dingoes share an animal family with dogs, but make no mistake—they're wild animals!

For thousands of years, Aborigines, or native peoples of Australia, have lived side by side with these canines. They created stories and artwork based on dingoes. Some people believe that these peoples brought dingoes to Australia from Southeast Asia. Other people think dingoes may have crossed a land bridge, or an area of dry land that's now underwater.

That's wild!
This Aboriginal artwork shows a picture of a dingo. These pictures may be nearly 15,000 years old!

Dingoes are great hunters. They're at the top of their food chain in Australia!

Definitely a Dingo

There are many wild dogs in the world. How can you tell if a wild dog is a dingo? Look at its features.

Dingoes look a lot like **domesticated** dogs. They have thin, strong bodies that are perfect for running. They have pointed ears that always stand up. Their fur is tan, golden, or reddish. Their tail often has a white tip. Dingoes can grow to be about 4 feet (1.2 m) long, with a 13-inch (33 cm) tail. They usually weigh up to around 35 pounds (16 kg).

That's wild!

American Dingoes, or Carolina Dogs, used to live in the wild of the American Southeast. Now, they're domesticated. They share many features with Australian dingoes.

carolina Dog

Some dingoes have black fur, but that's not common in Australia. Black dingoes are more common in Southeast Asia.

At Home in the Outback

When most people think of dingoes, they imagine all of them live in Australia. However, similar wild canines live in Southeast Asia, in countries such as Thailand, Indonesia, and the Philippines.

In Australia, dingoes live in a few different **habitats**. They're found mostly in the western and central **regions** of Australia. Some live in hot, wet places. Dingoes **thrive** in grasslands and forests, or even on islands. However, they're famous for being animals of the Australian outback, which is a large desert.

That's wild!
Australians built a fence to keep dingoes out of farmland in the southeastern part of the country. It's more than 3,488 miles (5,613 km) long!

Dingoes that live in the outback may wander for many miles each day to find water and food.

Dingo Families

Some dingoes are solitary, which means they hunt and live alone most of the time. However, many dingoes live in packs, which are often strong family units. They usually include a mother and father dingo and their young. A pack may have up to 12 dingoes in it.

Dingoes **communicate** with each other through howling. They make a great team while hunting. A pack of dingoes can bring down a much larger animal, such as a kangaroo.

That's wild!

The main female in a pack sometimes kills the young of other females. This ensures that her young will have enough food to eat.

Young dingoes in a pack will often fight each other to find out which one is the strongest.

A Dingo's Life

Dingoes often mate for life, which means the same male and female come together to make babies for as long as they live. Females usually have one litter of babies, called pups, every year. They usually give birth to the pups in a den, which can be in a hollow tree, a cave, or a **burrow**.

After the pups are born, the parents watch them carefully from a distance. They do this to make sure predators don't come near the den. The parents also feed the pups and teach them how to hunt.

That's wild!

Young male dingoes often live and hunt alone. They sometimes join a pack to hunt, but they're kicked out if there's not enough food to go around.

There are commonly four to six pups in each litter.

Dingo Diet

What's on the menu in the outback? Packs of dingoes may hunt large animals, such as kangaroos and wallabies. Dingoes hunting on their own may eat smaller **prey**, such as rats, mice, lizards, and rabbits.

Even though dingoes are carnivores, or meat-eaters, they will also eat nuts, fruits, and grains. They're known to eat livestock, or farm animals, such as sheep and cows. People often kill dingoes because of this, but most dingoes would rather find a wild meal!

Dingoes are smart animals. If they can't finish their food right away, they bury it to eat later!

That's wild!
Dingoes will also scavenge, or look around for dead animals and trash they can eat.

Hunting as a Team

Dingoes usually claim their own territory for hunting. They'll roam great distances looking for prey to hunt, even in the hot desert. They often hunt at night when it's cooler.

Dingoes that hunt alone might **ambush** small prey. Dingoes that hunt as a team have their own special hunting **techniques**. They might take turns chasing an animal until the prey is too tired to run anymore. The pack could also attack an animal from different directions.

That's wild!
Dingoes are known to go for the throat when they attack!

Dingo packs often surround their prey before attacking.

Adapting and Surviving

Over time, dingoes have **adapted** to habitats in Australia and Southeast Asia. Their adaptations help them not only live in the area but act as a top predator there.

Dingoes have great senses. Their pointed ears give them a great sense of hearing. Like other canines, dingoes have a great sense of smell. Their vision is also sharp, which helps them spot prey.

Another adaptation is their fur color. Golden and tan-colored dingoes blend into the dusty desert habitat. That's called camouflage.

That's wild!
Hunting as a pack is another great adaptation.

Dingoes survive well in many habitats because they're willing to eat almost anything!

Dingoes and People

Are dingoes **dangerous**? Like all wild dogs, dingoes sometimes become **aggressive** and attack people. However, this is uncommon. They'd rather hunt for smaller animals.

People have to be careful around dingoes. People started feeding and playing with dingoes on Fraser Island near eastern Queensland, Australia. The dingoes became comfortable with people and wanted their food. Over the years, there have been a few dingo attacks on this island. An adult human might be able to fight a dingo off, but a child probably couldn't.

That's wild!

In 2001, dingoes killed a nine-year-old boy on Fraser Island. Because of that, 31 dingoes were found and killed on the island.

If you see a dingo, stand still. You may call for help, but stay calm. Screaming and waving your arms might make the dingo aggressive.

Australia's Symbol

Dingoes have become a **symbol** of the Australian outback. Today, these wild canines are in trouble. People hunt them, and farmers kill them to keep their livestock safe.

The biggest risk to the dingo population is that dingoes mate with people's pet dogs. This makes more **hybrid** dingoes. People should keep their pets inside or in a fenced yard. This could save the pure dingo population in Australia! Hopefully, dingoes will roam the Australian outback for many years to come.

Glossary

adapt: To change in order to live better in a certain environment.

aggressive: Showing a readiness to attack.

ambush: To attack by surprise.

burrow: A hole an animal digs in the ground for shelter.

communicate: To share ideas and feelings through sounds and motions.

dangerous: Unsafe.

domesticated: Bred and raised for use by people.

habitat: The natural place where an animal or plant lives.

hybrid: The young of two animals of different kinds.

prey: An animal hunted by other animals for food.

region: A large area of land that has a number of features in common.

symbol: Something that stands for something else.

technique: A particular skill or ability that one uses to do something.

thrive: To grow successfully.

Index

Websites

Due to the changing nature of Internet links, PowerKids Press has developed an online list of websites related to the subject of this book. This site is updated regularly. Please use this link to access the list: www.powerkidslinks.com/canine/dingo